LIFE IS VERY GOOD

30 DAY DEVOTIONAL

CULTIVATING A LIFESTYLE OF WORSHIP

BY
ROBERT AND
JUANITA SANCHEZ

LIFE IS VERY GOOD

Published by:
Firstfruits Publishing
P.O. Box 3726
Merced, CA 95344
www.prophetrobsanchez.com/firstfruitspublishing

In Partnership with:
A Book's Mind
PO Box 272847
Fort Collins, CO 80527
www.abooksmind.com

ISBN 978-1-944255-25-1

Printed in the United States of America.

THIS DEVOTIONAL IS DEDICATED TO:

Our girls: Zoe, Hannah and Carly. You are gifts God has given to us and we pray you reach your full godly potential in this life. We hope we can truly be examples of having a worship lifestyle and always know that we love you.

(Juanita) I would like to give special thanks to 2 people. First, to my mom, Lidia Sanchez. You are the first person I sang with and I still enjoy singing with you. I've watched you throughout my entire life and have learned so much. You've been through struggles but you kept worshiping. You've dealt with sickness but you never lost your song. Even when you could have given up, you didn't. I'm very proud of you and I love you. Thank you for being my mom.

I also want to thank my first worship leader, Eliud Landin. You taught me how to work on a team, how to listen to and blend with other singers and reminded us to be aware of our facial expressions. But most importantly, you taught me to always follow the leading of the Holy Spirit. You may not have realized it, but you made an impact in my life. Thank you.

(Robert) I would like to give special thanks to Manuel Ochoa for being a friend and a spiritual father. You taught me how to pray, worship and meditate on the word of God. You poured into my life because you saw my potential, not only as a minister but as a prophet. I appreciate all the prayers and the time you invested. It helped lay the foundation of what I stand on today. I love and thank you.

DAY 1
TRUE IDENTITY

THROUGH THE POWER OF WORSHIP YOU BECOME MIGHTY, EVEN IN THE MIDST OF ADVERSITY. THE ANGEL APPEARED AND CALLED GIDEON A "MIGHTY MAN OF VALOR". GIDEON'S WORSHIP CAUSED THE ANGEL TO REVEAL WHO HE WAS IN GOD'S EYES. YOUR WORSHIP GIVES YOU IDENTITY.

LIFE IS VERY GOOD!

There are those who have been in the same position as Gideon: they thought of themselves as less than how God truly saw them. But when you step into worship, you walk into intimacy with the Heavenly Father and He helps you see clearly. You allow yourself to be transparent before Him, and He opens your eyes so you can see yourself as He sees you: fearfully and wonderfully made (Psalm 139:14). It's a great place to be in when someone else sees the potential within you and they encourage it to come out. Myles Munroe wrote, "You will never discover who you were meant to be if you use another person to find yourself. If you want to know who you are, look at God, look at the Creator, not the creation."[1]

There is potential locked up inside of you and worship releases the hand of God to show you what you are capable of doing. There are many people who don't realize their full potential, and because of it, they don't accomplish all that was in their heart. I once read that the greatest place to find potential is in a cemetery because there you will find thousands of people who had a dream but were never able to fulfill it. Don't allow that to happen in your life. Raise your hands and ask the Lord to fill you up with His glory and power to accomplish all that He sees in you. You are more than what you see in the mirror. Worship the Lord and let Him open your eyes to see your own potential. "For as he thinks in his heart, so is he" (Proverbs 23:7). Don't think of yourself as less. You are more than a conqueror and a mighty person of valor. See your true identity in Him.

The Lord says...

Your worship fills up My throne room and gives Me joy, for I enjoy hearing your voice as you lift it to Me. I have created you to be a worshiper. I have also created you in My image and likeness, so you are mighty and strong. Don't see yourself as less than what I have created you. Know who you are: you are Mine.

If you believe it, say oh yeah!

---

1 Munroe, Myles. *Potential for Every Day*. Shippensburg, PA: Destiny Image, 2008. Print.

You know my sitting down and my rising up; You understand my thought afar off. You comprehend my path and my lying down, And are acquainted with all my ways.

How precious also are Your thoughts to me, O God! How great is the sum of them! If I should count them, they would be more in number than the sand; When I awake, I am still with You.

(Psalms 139:2-3, 17-18)

DAY 2

WORSHIP THROUGH GIVING

WHEN YOU WORSHIP THE LORD WITH GIVING, IT WILL CAUSE YOUR ADVERSARY TO FEAR WHO YOU ARE. REMEMBER, GIDEON'S SACRIFICE RELEASED VICTORY TO ISRAEL AND CAUSED HIS ENEMIES TO SCATTER. SO ARISE AND WORSHIP, THE LORD HAS DELIVERED THE ENEMY INTO YOUR HANDS.

LIFE IS VERY GOOD!

It's always interesting to see the faces of people in church when the pastor begins to speak about giving. Either they are interested (because they are givers) or they tune the message out (because they feel giving is overly talked about or they aren't givers). What the latter group doesn't realize is the importance of giving and what it can do for them. Giving isn't just about finances; it's about every part of your life. Jesus taught in Luke 6:38 and said, "Give, and it will be given to you: good measure, pressed down, shaken together, and running over will be put into your bosom. For with the same measure that you use, it will be measured back to you." He never made a reference to finances, because he was teaching about life principles in general. If you give people respect, you will receive respect. If you give people a helping hand when they're in need, a helping hand will be extended to you. If you provide financial help to someone, one day someone will provide the financial breakthrough you need.

So in teaching about giving, not only does it apply to finances but it can also apply to worship as well. Hebrews 13:15 & 16 says to "offer the sacrifice of praise to God… for with such sacrifices God is well pleased." Many people in the Bible offered worship to the Lord, and because of their sacrifices God showed up on their behalf (1 Samuel 30:6-8; 2 Kings 3:12-18; 2 Chronicles 20:1-4). There were others who gave an offering as an act of worship and God provided for them as well (1 Kings 17:8-16; 2 Kings 4:1-7; Acts 9:36-41). This principle shows that when you give unto the Lord, He will give back to you and give you the victory in your circumstance. You don't have to fear the bill collectors, the illness or anything the adversary may try to use against you. Do as Gideon did: give everything you have to the Lord and He will step into your situation and cause all opposition to flee.

The Lord says…

My Word is true and will fulfill what I spoke it to do. Because you have been grafted into the lineage of Abraham, the promises I gave to him can also be received by you. When you stand on my foundation and believe My Word, it will become life to you and give you victory. I want you to be blessed. I want you to succeed. Follow My principles and the rest will fall into place. Give unto Me and I'll give back unto you, in abundance.

If you believe it, say oh yeah!

Give unto the LORD, O you mighty ones, Give unto the LORD glory and strength. Give unto the LORD the glory due to His name; Worship the LORD in the beauty of holiness.

(Psalms 29:1-2)

DAY 3

VICTORY IN WORSHIP

REMEMBER THIS: THE POWER OF YOUR WORSHIP WILL DEFEAT YOUR ADVERSARY. GIDEON'S 300 MEN, ARMED WITH A TRUMPET (PRAISE), A TORCH (THE LIGHT OF GOD), AND THE WORD OF THE LORD, DID WHAT 32,000 MEN COULD NOT DO: DEFEAT THEIR ENEMIES. CORPORATE PRAISES RELEASE HIS VICTORY.

LIFE IS VERY GOOD!

The Word says in Leviticus 26:8, "Five of you shall chase a hundred, and a hundred of you shall put ten thousand to flight." There is strength in numbers, and quality is just as important sometimes more important than quantity. Gideon learned that God was looking for quality men who would worship and shine a light into victory. Even Jesus knew this and that's why he wanted to impart into 12 men who would then impart into 70, who would impart into 300, who would slowly impart into the world. That is how change takes place: one person at a time. On your own, you can accomplish some things, but when you come together as a corporate body, you can accomplish much. And when you all come together in one accord, something powerful can take place. God can work through many people and also through a few.

Praise and worship works in the same manner. When people come together with the common goal of singing praises to God, the atmosphere that is created is contagious. It breaks strongholds, heals diseases, brings people to their knees in repentance and brings freedom to those oppressed and depressed. And that presence can be felt in a stadium of 32,000, a congregation of 300 or in the stillness of your prayer closet because wherever there is worship, the enemy has to flee. If he's not getting the attention, the enemy has no interest in being around. Therefore, lift up your voice in praise, especially if you have others joining you. Tell the enemy he has been defeated, and you're going to praise and worship about it until there is no longer breath in your lungs.

The Lord says…

With one word, I created the entire world and all that exists. With one act, I defeated the devil and took back the keys of death, hell and the grave. Because you were made in My image and likeness, you also have the power to change your circumstances with your words and your praise. Your praise will cause chains to break, and when you stand together with the Body, so much more can happen for My Kingdom. You're all important because together, you are stronger and with Me on your side, you are unstoppable!

If you believe it, say oh yeah!

Praise the LORD! I will praise the LORD with my whole heart, In the assembly of the upright and in the congregation. The works of the LORD are great, Studied by all who have pleasure in them.

(Psalms 111:1-2)

DAY 4
SHAKE IT OFF

TO THOSE WHO FEEL WEARY FROM THE JOURNEY, REMEMBER, GOD PROMISED REST TO YOU AND THAT WORD WILL NOT FAIL. RISE UP, SHAKE OFF ALL HEAVINESS AND LIFT UP A SHOUT OF PRAISE. THERE IS NO ONE LIKE OUR GOD.

LIFE IS VERY GOOD!

My grandmother (Nana, as we call her) has had dementia for the last several years. It's progressed to the point where she doesn't recognize me or Rob, our girls even less. When my mom goes to visit her at the home, Nana will sometimes talk about how she's ready to go at any time God wants to take her. She says her body gets tired and always reminds us to never get old. Although Nana's physical mind has forgotten many things, such as people or events, her spirit has never forgotten how to praise. She spends much of the visit (and the majority of her day) singing old hymns from her childhood. At 92 years of age, though her body has grown weary from her journey in this life, her spirit always lifts up a song of worship that gives her strength to continue each day.

It was never promised that life would be easy, but God did promise that He would never leave you (Hebrews 13:5). You can rest assured that His Word is true. Whatever you may be going through, God will not give you more than you can handle. Don't complain about your circumstances; give Him a praise in the midst of them. Your shout of praise will give you strength to endure and your song of worship will cause the walls around you to fall. Rest in the presence of the Lord and shake off the heaviness of this life, for in His presence is fullness of joy.

The Lord says…

As you lift up a shout or song of praise unto My Name, My joy will fill you up to overflowing. I will give you strength to rise over any circumstance, peace to calm the storms, and joy to counter any sorrow. I will not give you more than you can handle and when you place your burdens on Me, I have promised to give you rest. I love you more than you know and My desire is for you to have the best. Stand on My Word and find your strength in Me. I am always with you.

If you believe it, say oh yeah!

Commit your way to the Lord, Trust also in Him, And He shall bring it to pass. He shall bring forth your righteousness as the light, And your justice as the noonday. Rest in the Lord, and wait patiently for Him…

(Psalm 37:5-7)

DAY 5
THE BLESSING OF UNITED WORSHIP

ARE YOU READY FOR HIS GLORY TO FILL YOUR HOUSE? IF SO, REMEMBER THIS: IT WILL COME TO PASS WHEN YOUR SONG OF WORSHIP & YOUR SHOUT OF PRAISE BECOME ONE, DECLARING THAT THE LORD IS GOOD. GET READY; HIS CLOUD IS ABOUT TO POUR OUT HIS MERCY OVER YOU.

LIFE IS VERY GOOD!

Everyone has their own way of expressing joy. Some people jump, some people smile, while others laugh or even cry. But when all come together in expressing the joy of the Lord, something special happens. In Psalm 133, David talked about how the blessing flowed when "brethren dwell together in unity" (verse 1). In verse 3, it says, "For there the LORD commanded the blessing— Life forevermore." For *there* the Lord commands the blessing. Where is *there*? It is within unity, and there is no greater unity than a people who worship together. It has the power to change the outcome of situations. It can tear down giant walls that stand before you. It can break prison chains and open doors. It can bring freedom physically, mentally and emotionally. And it brings God's blessing.

The word *blessing* means prosperity (Strongs H1293) and its meaning comes from the root 'to kneel' (Strongs H1288). When we kneel before the Lord and bless Him as a body, we bring glory to His Name. God in turn, pours out His blessing, or His prosperity, over us. We can succeed, flourish and thrive in every area of our life because of our united praise and worship lifted up to the throne room.

God meant for us to enjoy fellowship and worship together; we weren't meant to be alone (Genesis 2:18a). This is why God created man (for God) and then why God created woman (for man). And it's why God pours out blessing when we are united in worship; our hearts are knit together with one another and with Him. There is covenant made in the atmosphere of worship, and within covenant there is life forevermore. Let His glory fill you up as you join with others in His presence.

The Lord says...

I desire to fill every part of your life with My presence. As you join with My body, My children, My bride and lift up praise, I will pour over you blessings that you can't contain. My blessings will satisfy, they will renew, they will heal and they will prosper you. Come together in one accord and see My glory fill you up to overflowing.

If you believe it, say oh yeah!

...indeed it came to pass, when the trumpeters and singers were as one, to make one sound to be heard in praising and thanking the LORD, and when they lifted up their voice with the trumpets and cymbals and instruments of music, and praised the LORD, saying: "For He is good, For His mercy endures forever," that the house, the house of the LORD, was filled with a cloud, so that the priests could not continue ministering because of the cloud; for the glory of the LORD filled the house of God.

(2 Chronicles 5:13-14)

DAY 6
POSITIVE PRAISE

WHEN YOUR HEART IS FLOODED WITH HIS PRESENCE, YOUR MOUTH WILL BE FILLED WITH LAUGHTER & YOUR LIPS WILL REJOICE WITH HIS PRAISES. SPEAK BLESSING & LET THE OVERFLOW BEGIN.

LIFE IS VERY GOOD!

"For out of the abundance of the heart the mouth speaks" (Matthew 12:34). It's a simple concept, and it's the reason why we have to use wisdom when we speak. Our tongues have the ability to encourage and build up, but it also has the ability to condemn and tear down. It all hinges on what you have in your heart. When you carry the joy of the Lord, it will give you strength for the day and hope for your life. Your outlook on life will be optimistic. Those will then be the words you speak.

Have you heard the question: is your glass half-empty or half-full? Even researchers have been interested in this idea of thinking and speaking positively and the possible link it has to better health. In a web article, the MAYO Clinic stated that possible health benefits may include increased life span, lower rates of depression and distress, and better coping skills during hardships.[2] When your heart is joyful, your words are joyful, and your life is joyful. That's a definite reason to give God praise!

Many people may think having a positive outlook on life is naive, but when you have the Lord in your life, He helps you look at your situations in a different way. You don't ignore the tribulations that come, you just face them with a different mindset. The Word says to "count it all joy when you fall into various trials, knowing that the testing of your faith produces patience... that you may be perfect and complete, lacking nothing" (James 1:2-4). To *count* is to number, consider or regard[3], which is to think carefully about or believe. So you should think about your trials and hardships as times of joy, times that will build up your strength and patience, times that will give you something to praise the Lord about, times that will cause you to worship. And when the joy of the Lord overflows from your life, and His praises flow from your lips, it will pour out on those around you and hopefully cause them to change their outlook as well. Ephesians 4:29 says, "Let no corrupt word proceed out of your mouth, but what is good for necessary edification, that it may impart grace to the hearers." What flows from your mouth (and

2 Mayo Clinic Staff. "Stress Management." *Positive Thinking: Reduce Stress by Eliminating Negative Self-talk.* Mayo Clinic, 4 March, 2014. Web.

3 "Dictionary.com - The World's Favorite Online English Dictionary!" *Dictionary.com.* 2016. Web.

in reality, from your heart) not only impacts your life, but the lives of those around you. Speak life, grace and blessings to yourself and to others and watch the glory of the Lord manifest all around you.

The Lord says...

You have the power of death and life in your tongue so use that power to edify your brothers and sisters. You have the ability to change lives with the words you speak because they are My words of life flowing from you. Allow My Spirit to fill your heart and transform you into a greater person. My life and everything it contains was meant to be given to My children so they can experience freedom in Me. Do not keep My joy trapped within you; let it out and cause others to feel the same.

If you believe it, say oh yeah!

You shall eat in plenty and be satisfied, and praise the name of the
Lord your God, who has dealt wondrously with you;
And My people shall never be put to shame.

(Joel 2:26)

DAY 7
FALL INTO ALIGNMENT

WHEN YOUR HEART IS IN ALIGNMENT WITH GOD, YOU WILL HAVE A SHOUT FOR JOY. WHEN YOUR HEART IS OUT OF ALIGNMENT, IT WILL BEAR MANY SORROWS. TRUST IN THE LORD AND ALLOW HIS MERCY TO SURROUND YOU.

LIFE IS VERY GOOD!

I go to the chiropractor on a regular basis. With as much traveling that we do in the car and plane, it helps to keep my body working in the way it's supposed to. Plus, I can feel when my back is out of alignment, and it doesn't feel good. Whenever I'm misaligned, I can feel soreness and pain in that area, and all I want to do is get an adjustment. The pain is uncomfortable until I finally get to the chiropractor. I put my trust in the capable hands of someone who I know can help me. It works the same way in the spiritual realm.

Jesus wants you to be aligned with Him so you can see what He sees, hear what He hears, and realize the vision He has for your life. This is why worship is so important. When you worship the Lord, your focus is on Him and only Him. Nothing else should matter. Worship helps you open up your spirit to receive His infilling. When you aren't standing with Christ, or when you're out of alignment, you're standing against Him or in His way. This is the reason He rebuked Peter in Mark 8:31-33. Peter couldn't understand why Jesus would have to suffer and "be killed," so he "took [Jesus] aside and began to rebuke Him." Jesus turned around in verse 33 and said, "Get behind Me, Satan! For you are not mindful of the things of God, but the things of men." Jesus didn't call Peter Satan because He thought Peter was the devil at that moment. Jesus knew He was on the earth for a purpose, and that purpose was to die for the sins of the world. He didn't want anyone trying to deter Him because that act carried great meaning. Though it seemed like it would be a sad event, in reality, the eternal significance was going to carry great joy. Jesus wanted Peter to trust God, and in what His plan was. He wants you to do the same. Keep in alignment with the plan of God, no matter how uncomfortable or painful it may be, because in the end, you will have a mighty praise in your mouth.

The Lord says...

Trust in the plan I have for you and lift up a praise to Me. When you stand with Me, you will have new vision for your life because you will see with My eyes and hear with My ears. Don't allow your heart to wander but follow Me whole-heartedly. I have the best intentions for you. I will surround you with My mercy and shower you with My grace. I will open up the pathway before you and walk with

You all the way. Praise Me in the good times and bad, during the ups and downs, and watch My goodness overflow in all areas of your life.

If you believe it, say oh yeah!

Trust in the LORD with all your heart, And lean not on your own understanding; In all your ways acknowledge Him, And He shall direct your paths. Do not be wise in your own eyes; Fear the LORD and depart from evil. It will be health to your flesh, And strength to your bones.

(Proverbs 3:5-8)

DAY 8
THE MUSICAL CALLED LIFE

HOW DO YOU CHANGE THE CIRCUMSTANCES THAT SURROUND YOUR LIFE? BY BREAKING FORTH IN A SONG, REJOICING & SINGING PRAISES. IT'S TIME TO MAKE A JOYFUL NOISE & LET ALL THE EARTH HEAR YOUR SHOUT OF PRAISE, FOR HE IS WORTHY.

LIFE IS VERY GOOD!

I love musicals; I always have. Whether it's watching one on television or live at the theatre, there's something about them that I enjoy. I'm sure it has a lot to do with the music and the stories they tell. Growing up in a musical family, it's a natural thing for it to be a part of my life. Imagine if real life were a musical. At particular points in your life, all of a sudden you would begin to sing a song that would bring more meaning and help explain whatever situation you were going through. At some points, life would play out as a comedy, other times it might be dramatic or even a tragedy. Sometimes it would be a solo while other times, people might join in with you.

You may giggle while reading this but life IS somewhat of a musical. How often do you go into your car and your favorite cd is playing? You walk into the elevator at work and music is on. You go for a jog and there's a specific playlist you use. Your teenager gets upset at something you said so they slam the door to their room and crank up the radio. You may even need the relaxing sounds to help you sleep at night. When you really think about it, music engulfs everything we do but that's how God created it to be. David wrote in Psalm 8:2, "Out of the mouth of babes and nursing infants You have ordained strength." The word *strength* in this scripture means majesty or praise (Strongs H5797). God wanted praise to be a part of your life, and David is a great example of a musical life. When times were great, David sang. When times were difficult, David sang. When people hated him and wanted to kill him, David sang. When he felt joy, peaceful, lonely, or afraid, David sang. Practically the entire book of Psalms depicts David's ups and downs, and everything in between, in musical form. Through song, David was able to express his feelings and what he was going through, but at the same time, come to an understanding that God was always in control and He had the power to change the circumstances surrounding him. It didn't matter if he was alone or in the sanctuary, David always found a way to lift up his voice unto the Lord His God. Praise and worship changed David's point of view toward trials and tribulations by taking his eyes off himself and focusing them on God. It can do that for you too.

So the next time you find yourself singing a little tune while doing housework or homework, just smile and keep singing knowing God is probably singing along with you. He's going to see you through.

The Lord says…

If I care for the flowers of the field and the birds of the air, how much more is My love for you? I enjoy when I hear you lift up a song of worship to Me in your secret place and when you praise in the church together with the Body. I hear when you cry out to Me in desperation or in pain. I will sing over you My songs of peace and love to comfort, to lift you up and fill you with joy unspeakable and full of glory.

If you believe it, say oh yeah!

Thus Israel saw the great work which the Lord had done in Egypt; so the people feared the Lord, and believed the Lord and His servant Moses.

Then Moses and the children of Israel sang this song to the Lord, and spoke, saying:

"I will sing to the Lord, For He has triumphed gloriously! The horse and its rider He has thrown into the sea! The Lord is my strength and song, And He has become my salvation; He is my God, and I will praise Him; My father's God, and I will exalt Him."

(Exodus 14:31-15:2)

DAY 9
JUST STAND UP AND PRAISE

To be joyful in your soul means to be loose & free to celebrate God's great work. It's like every bone in your body is laughing, singing, & declaring His goodness. Joy is more than an emotion, it's His strength.

Life is very good!

I enjoy celebrating with another person, whether it's for a birthday, a graduation or the birth of a child. Rejoicing with others is a wonderful thing to do, and I think it's more enjoyable doing it with people you know and care about rather than just by yourself. When you celebrate and have fun, you don't really care who is watching. I see that in children all the time. Kids can be singing a song all by themselves but once others join in, the jumping and craziness begins. Children are free in who they are and what they are doing. And that's how God wants you celebrate.

King David was the type of person who sang and praised like he was the only one in the room, yet he did this whether he was alone or in the company of his people; it was his lifestyle. And God was pleased with his type of praise, so much so that when David's wife Michal "despised him in her heart" (2 Samuel 6:16) and criticized David for "uncovering himself…as one of the base fellows shamelessly uncovers himself" (verse 20), God didn't allow Michal to bear any children "to the day of her death" (verse 23). God loves when you freely worship Him! Don't worry about what others think or say; the important thing is what God thinks and says. When you worship Him with all of your being, it causes the Father to smile down on you. He's pleased when you give Him all of yourself, not just a part.

"You've gotta dance like there's nobody watching,

Love like you'll never be hurt,

Sing like there's nobody listening,

And live like it's heaven on earth."

-William W. Purkey

The Lord says…

Lift up your voice and sing, lift up your hands and praise, lift up your heart and worship. I, the Lord, am pleased as you give all of yourself to Me for I gave all of Myself to you on Calvary. My death was to give you life and freedom in abundance. Let your worship extend to the far reaches of the earth and others will join with you in a symphony that will give a fragrant aroma in My throne room. Let who I am within you be released as you worship in My presence.

If you believe it, say oh yeah!

Bless the Lord, O my soul; And all that is within me, bless His holy name!

(Psalm 103:1)

DAY 10
ALONE BUT NEVER ALONE

THE WAY TO OVERCOME THE SEASON OF TROUBLE IS TO FIND A STILL, QUIET PLACE AND ALLOW YOUR PRAYER AND PRAISE TO ASCEND TO A NEW HEIGHT. YOU CAN CALL UPON HIS NAME AND HE WILL DELIVER YOU. AS YOUR WORSHIP GOES UP, THE POWER AND ANSWERS FLOW DOWN.

LIFE IS VERY GOOD!

Ecclesiastes 3 says there is a season and a time for everything. Verse 5 specifically says, "A time to embrace, and a time to refrain from embracing." There are times in life when you need people around you: to support you in times of need, to rally around you when you need extra encouragement, to help you when you are stuck. These are times when the gathering of the saints gives strength, joy and love. But there are other times when you just need to be alone. Words don't bring comfort and hugs don't bring relief. The only thing that satisfies is the all-encompassing presence of God.

David knew this to be a truth. There were many times when David felt alone and all he could do was call on the name of the Lord. Yet even when David felt like no one understood him, he knew God was always there. He prayed, "Where can I go from Your Spirit? Or where can I flee from Your presence? If I ascend into heaven, You are there; If I make my bed in hell, behold, You are there... I will praise You, for I am fearfully and wonderfully made; Marvelous are Your works, And that my soul knows very well" (Psalms 139:7-8,14). In the ups and downs, David could always count on his Heavenly Father being there and answering his cries. God was always faithful to David and God is faithful to you, even in seasons of trouble. Sometimes all it takes is to find a quiet place and begin to worship Him.

In Genesis 28:10, Jacob was running from his brother Esau, from whom he stole the blessing. Scared, alone and fearing for his life, Jacob stopped somewhere between Beersheba and Haran and decided to lay down to sleep. "And he dreamed, and behold a ladder set up on the earth, and the top of it reached to heaven: and behold the angels of God ascending and descending on it" (Genesis 28:12). In this dream, God spoke to Jacob and gave him a promise for his future, not just Jacob's but also for the generations following him. God said, "Behold, I am with you and will keep you wherever you go" (verse 15). How was it that God was able to speak to Jacob in the midst of the turmoil going on in his life? Jacob had put himself in a solitary place and when he decided to rest, he placed a rock under his head. The rock signified the solid foundation of Christ. In his dark time of trouble, Jacob couldn't think clearly so he placed his thoughts, his intellect, and his will on the strength only the Lord could provide. Jacob realized God was with him the whole time, and his dream confirmed his revelation. The angels took Jacob's prayers and praise to the heavens, and brought down God's promise of a bright future. So don't worry when trials seem to surround you. Put your mind on Christ, lift up your voice and begin to praise the Lord for His goodness. He'll give you a new perspective and assure you of His presence that will never leave you.

The Lord says...

In your times of trouble, you don't need to be in a church full of people in order to find My presence. When you separate yourself in prayer and lift up your praises to Me, I will always answer you. My hand will guide and lead you to the place you need to be. Don't worry about the circumstance, for I am greater than the circumstance. Don't worry about the problem, for I have already delivered you from the problem. As long as you get alone with Me, I will shine My presence over you and be the answer to your question.

If you believe it, say oh yeah!

He who dwells in the secret place of the Most High
Shall abide under the shadow of the Almighty.

Because he has set his love upon Me, therefore I will deliver him; I will set him on high, because he has known My name. He shall call upon Me, and I will answer him; I will be with him in trouble; I will deliver him and honor him.

(Psalms 91:1, 14-15)

DAY 11
IN THE BEST AND WORST OF TIMES

When you face adversity, the atmosphere you create will deliver you. When his men spoke of stoning him after the battle at Ziklag, David's worship created an atmosphere of change and caused God to speak a promise: pursue, overtake and without fail, recover all. His promise declares success.

Life is very good!

King David was the type of person who always placed God first in his life. He had a very intimate relationship with His Heavenly Father; it was special. That's why God specifically chose David to be king over the people of Israel, because he was "a man after His own heart" (1 Samuel 13:14). When David rejoiced, he worshiped. When he was confused, he worshiped. When his heart was broken, he worshiped. David knew that in the presence of God, things changed. Even after the death of his infant son in 2 Samuel 12:20, David still "went into the house of the LORD and worshiped." This is what happened at Ziklag.

David and his men had come home from a battle to find the entire city of Ziklag burned and all the women and children taken captive. Instead of going and fighting the Amalekites, David did nothing, or seemingly nothing. I'm sure David's lack of desire to retaliate angered his soldiers greatly. In their minds, David wasn't doing enough. But he was doing more than they realized. He went and "strengthened himself in the LORD his God" (1 Samuel 30:6). He did what would later be written in verse 33 of Matthew 6: "But seek first the kingdom of God and His righteousness, and all these things shall be added to you." David decided to worship the Lord and find the answers to his questions. He first entered into the presence of God because without the Lord with him and his men, they would not defeat the enemy. David found peace within worship and when his soul came to rest, he asked the Lord, "Shall I pursue this troop? Shall I overtake them?" God answered him with a promise, "Pursue, for you shall surely overtake them and without fail recover all" (1 Samuel 30:8). How awesome is the Lord!

Your worship can have the same impact on your situations also. God is not a respecter of persons; if He did it for David, He will do it for you. Your worship is powerful when you lift your heart fully to the Lord. God is on your side and He will never leave you alone. Turn your adversity into victory by shouting a loud praise! Turn your hardships into blessings by seeing them as joy and thanking God for them. Your life can turn out different from how it first started when you learn to strengthen yourself in His presence and lay everything down at His feet.

The Lord says…

My promise to you is to pursue, overtake and recover all without fail, just as it was for My servant David. When you come into My presence, I will give you all you are looking for and answer the questions which may be in your heart. I have My best in store for you and your worship unlocks that. When your praises come up to My throne room, My blessings pour out upon you. Know that I receive your praises and your worship. It pleases Me to be in communion with you.

If you believe it, say oh yeah!

The Lord is my shepherd; I shall not want. He makes me to lie down in green pastures; He leads me beside the still waters. He restores my soul; He leads me in the paths of righteousness for His name's sake. Yea, though I walk through the valley of the shadow of death, I will fear no evil; For You are with me; Your rod and Your staff, they comfort me. You prepare a table before me in the presence of my enemies; You anoint my head with oil; My cup runs over. Surely goodness and mercy shall follow me all the days of my life; And I will dwell in the house of the Lord Forever.

(Psalm 23:1-6)

DAY 12
DON'T RUN AWAY, RUN TO HIM

When we find ourselves in the midst of trying times, we feel alone and search for a way out. But to feel close to God, we don't have to climb the highest mountain. When you lift Him up, He will exalt you. Go ahead, give Him the highest praise.

Life is very good!

Sometimes the easiest thing for people to do when they go through difficult periods is to retreat and try to solve the problems on their own. At times it works but many times it doesn't. This is because God created you to fellowship with others, not be an island unto yourself. You may say, "I can do this myself," but remember, life is not a simple home improvement project like painting a room. God doesn't want you to do it alone. Many times I have to remind myself of that. I try to take on so many projects by myself, I end up burning out. The more efficient way is to ask someone for help. Don't walk through difficult times alone. Know that Christ is with you. Though you may feel alone during trying times, you aren't.

But you are not the only one who has faced difficulties. The prophet Elijah did great miracles and gave many prophetic words that came to pass, but even with the highs, there were lows in his life. One low, in particular, came after a powerful victory by the hand of God. In 1 Kings 18, Elijah confronted 450 prophets of Baal on Mount Carmel by challenging their god to show up by fire. The prophets of Baal prayed, cried out, and began cutting themselves, but nothing made a difference. Elijah prepared his sacrifice, and then proceeded to drench it with water several times. When Elijah called on the Lord, "The fire of the Lord fell and consumed the burnt sacrifice, and the wood and the stones and the dust, and it licked up the water that was in the trench" (1 Kings 18:38). All the prophets of Baal were taken to the Brook Kishon and killed. This was definitely one of the highlights of Elijah's ministry, but it was short-lived. Once Jezebel heard about what happened to her prophets, she threatened to kill Elijah. One moment he stood victorious against the prophets of Baal, while the next he ran away when one woman made a threat. Obviously, running away never solves anything. You still have to deal with the problem when you return. How much better is it to cry out to Jesus, your help in times of trouble? He is your refuge and strength when you don't know what to do.

You need to realize that God is everywhere you are. His desire is to help His people be blessed. He knows your life will endure trials and tribulations but His hand will guide you through them all. Never feel like you have to solve your problems on your own. And when you feel like no one knows what you are going through, draw close to God and He will draw close to you (James 4:8). Though

Elijah ran away from Jezebel and isolated himself, God assured him of His presence. It wasn't in the strong wind nor the earthquake nor the fire. It was in the "still small voice" (1 Kings 19:12). All you need to do is worship God and His voice will speak to you. You don't have to go to a mountain or to a church; wherever you are, He is also. Lift up a praise in the midst of your prayer and He will answer. Rest in that.

The Lord says…

Search for Me and I will be found. Call out My Name and I will respond. Though you may try to run away from your problems and trials, know that I am always with you in the midst of them. You don't need to fear being alone. I am always there to bring comfort and peace, for I am the Comforter and the Prince of Peace. My love will surround you and I will give you the answers you need.

If you believe it, say oh yeah!

My soul, wait silently for God alone, For my expectation is from Him. He only is my rock and my salvation; He is my defense; I shall not be moved. In God is my salvation and my glory; The rock of my strength, And my refuge, is in God. Trust in Him at all times, you people; Pour out your heart before Him; God is a refuge for us.

(Psalm 62:5-8)

DAY 13
PRAISING IN FAITH

REMEMBER: WHEN YOU NEED WALLS OF OPPOSITION TO FALL & THE SEASON TO CHANGE, ALLOW YOUR PRAISE TO BECOME A MIGHTY SHOUT. WHEN ISRAEL SHOUTED AS ONE MAN AT THE SOUND OF THE SHOFAR, THE WALLS FELL FLAT AND THEY WENT IN & TOOK THE CITY. YOUR SHOUT GIVES YOU WHAT GOD PROMISED! IT'S TIME TO TAKE YOUR LAND.

LIFE IS VERY GOOD!

It's hard to imagine a giant wall falling down because of a shout, but that's exactly what happened at Jericho in Joshua 6. God promised the children of Israel a place of their own, the land that had been promised to Abraham, Isaac and Jacob, a land of milk and honey. He delivered them out of Egypt, brought them through the wilderness and now they were on the edge of their promised land. They believed in what God promised them but they had to put action to the words. It wasn't enough to just have faith in God. James 2:12 says, "Faith without works is dead." A dream will only be a dream unless you put work into fulfilling it. A business plan will never become a business unless the necessary steps are taken to ensure a successful startup. This is the point where many fall short.

People will receive a word from the Lord and they praise God for it. Then they sit and wait for something to happen. They expect God to do all the work because He gave the word. And when circumstances arise that seem to block the fulfillment of the word, they feel either the word was wrong or they lose hope. Don't allow this to happen to you! "And let us not be weary in well doing: for in due season we shall reap, if we faint not" (Galatians 6:9 KJV). When you see the walls against you, continue to worship and give thanks to the Lord. He wants to know how far you're willing to go to hold the promise in your hands. The word will come to pass, as long as you continue to believe and put "feet to your faith".

The children of Israel needed the walls of Jericho to fall in order for them to take the city. To do this, they had to follow instructions. Joshua placed the warriors in front, followed by the priests with the trumpets. And as they came into unity — voices and trumpets, faith and worship — what stood before them came down. The opposition didn't look so fierce once the walls became rubble. Let your worship and praise be grounded in faith, and always be in your heart. Then, watch the promises of God manifest before you.

The Lord says...

My Word will never return void and it will accomplish what I have declared, especially in your life. My power is in you and you can bring down anything that opposes you. The faith of My Son (Galatians 2:20 KJV) is in you and you can believe for those things which I have promised you. As you worship, you will find yourself strengthened in Me. Your voice and your declaration will move mountains. Never fear in the midst of trials for I abide in you and there is nothing too difficult for Me.

If you believe it, say oh yeah!

But let all those rejoice who put their trust in You;
Let them ever shout for joy, because You defend them;
Let those also who love Your name
Be joyful in You.

(Psalm 5:11)

DAY 14
CHRIST'S IMAGE IN YOU

If you don't learn to put on the image of Christ through worship, you will put on the image of everything else that surrounds you. Your attitude is a fruit of your environment. Let your atmosphere be filled with His praise, and allow His image to shine through you.

Life is very good!

"So God created man in His own image; in the image of God He created him; male and female He created them." This verse in Genesis 1:27 tells how man was specifically created to look just like God. Yet in Genesis 3, Adam decided to take off the image he was created in and walk in the earthly image he was formed from. He and Eve both believed the lie that they would look like God, instead of knowing they were already made in His image! The same can be said about you.

Throughout your life, you have heard many things that have had an impact on how you live today. I wish every child was able to hear someone tell them, "You is kind. You is smart. You is important". I know it's a quote from a movie[4] but the premise stands on its own. So many people hear the opposite growing up and they believe the lies they are told. They believe they are ugly. They believe they aren't smart. They believe they will always fail. And then those same people live their life with the stigma that their lives are worth nothing. Their environment has become a product of the image they placed on themselves, the image they decided to believe. It's time to turn it around and believe something new. It's time to worship the Lord and put on His image. From the beginning, God's plan was for you to look like Him, and throughout the bible, God reinforced His statement. Romans 8:37 calls you "more than conquerors through Him." First Peter 2:9 says you are a "chosen generation, a royal priesthood, a holy nation, His own special people, that you may proclaim the praises of Him who called you out of darkness into His marvelous light," and Revelation 1:6 says He has made you "kings and priests to His God and Father." But receiving the new means you have to let go of the old. For some, that's a difficult thing to do. But for those who want transformation, letting go is easy.

Bartimaeus had no problem walking away from the old opinions that held him down. He was a beggar and was blind; this was his reality. His name meant 'son of the unclean' (Strongs G924), so all his life Bartimaeus had to hear that the reason he was blind was because his family line was impure, not holy. When he heard Jesus was passing where he was, "He began to cry out and say, 'Jesus, Son

4 *The Help.* Dreamworks, 2011. Film.

of David, have mercy on me!'" (Mark 10:47) Many felt he didn't deserve to be heard so they quieted him down. But Bartimaeus wanted his life to change. He was probably tired of begging and wanted a better life. I'm sure he was sick of people's condescending opinions and attitudes. He wanted something different, so he cried out to the one person he knew could provide what he was looking for. When Jesus called for him, he threw off his garment and went (verse 50). The mantle that others had placed on Bartimaeus was broken off because he believed in faith and wasn't ashamed to ask for what he wanted. That faith opened the door for his healing. When he received it, Bartimaeus "immediately… followed Jesus on the road" (verse 52). He became a follower, but more important, he became a worshiper. Bartimaeus broke the limitations others had placed over him and changed his environment. You can do the same. If you want your surroundings to change, begin to see yourself differently and declare what you want. Surround yourself in worship and stand in faith, knowing that God can do anything, even the things that look impossible. Let the image you see in the mirror be the one God intended for you: Christ in you, the hope of glory (Colossians 1:27).

The Lord says…

I have placed Myself in you and you carry Me wherever you go. No matter what happens, you have been created in My image and likeness and that will never change. You are important to me. Don't allow others' opinions to change My image of you. My Words are true and uplifting. Let them fill your heart and spirit, and have them flow out of your mouth to transform the atmosphere around you.

If you believe it, say oh yeah!

For You formed my inward parts; You covered me in my mother's womb. I will praise You, for I am fearfully and wonderfully made;
Marvelous are Your works, And that my soul knows very well.

(Psalm 139:13-14)

DAY 15
WORSHIP WILL BE YOUR PROTECTION

In the time of conflict, we're always looking for a way to defend ourselves. As King Saul pursued David, he went to the priest and asked for a weapon. The priest said they only had the sword of Goliath, wrapped in something more important: the ephod. David's greatest weapon was always his power of worship. Find yourself in His refuge of peace as you praise Him. In Him, you've already won.

Life is very good!

Everyone has strengths in their life. You take your strengths and use them in different areas: at school, at work, at church. They can be your weapons in the midst of trials and tribulations. You use them to solve problems. And although we are all different and have unique personalities, we have one thing in common: we were made to worship. In Isaiah 43, God spoke how we were created and formed with a purpose. "Fear not, for I have redeemed you; I have called you by your name; You are Mine… Everyone who is called by My name, Whom I have created for My glory; I have formed him, yes, I have made him" (Verse 1, 7). You were created to give God all the glory and honor due His Name. When you do that, it not only blesses Him, but it blesses you as well. As children of God, He wants you to have all He's promised. He wants you to be victorious; that's why He declared it to be so. For this reason, you need to use the power of your worship in every circumstance.

David was known as a warrior, but above that, he was known as a worshiper. That's why God hand-picked him to rule Israel. He was a "man after [God's] own heart" (1 Samuel 13:14). Though he used a sling and a stone, David's other weapons were his voice and his instruments. So it's not surprising that David chose to use the sword of Goliath because it was wrapped in the priestly ephod. The ephod represents the image of God that is placed over your life. When you worship as a priest before the Lord, His image manifests in you and through you. You don't have to fight your battles for the Lord is your shield and buckler (Psalm 91:4). You don't have to worry about your finances because the Lord is your supplier and He has more than enough to meet your needs (Philippians 4:19). Trials will come, but when you use your weapon of worship, your ability to endure the trials becomes easier. What you have in your hand will become that much more powerful because of His image surrounding you. You may not have the sword of Goliath, but you do have another sword at your disposal: the sword of the Spirit, which is the word of God (Ephesians 6:17). You are prepared for anything that may come your way.

Allow those strengths to take root in your life, use them to tear down any wall that opposes you and praise your way through.

The Lord says…

I am your all in all. I am your protector and your refuge. I am your foundation and your strong tower. I will stand with you in the midst of your battles and when you are tired, lean on Me and I will carry you the rest of the way. Stand firm in who I am and see My hand work in your life. My will is for you to succeed, and as you worship, you will find My strength to make it through.

If you believe it, say oh yeah!

I will love You, O Lord, my strength. The Lord is my rock and my fortress and my deliverer; My God, my strength, in whom I will trust; My shield and the horn of my salvation, my stronghold. I will call upon the Lord, who is worthy to be praised; So shall I be saved from my enemies.

(Psalms 18:1-3)

DAY 16
IS YOUR PRAISE GREATER THAN YOUR COMPLAINT?

SOMETIMES IN THE MIDST OF OUR TRIALS, WE DIMINISH THE GREAT WORK GOD IS DOING IN OUR LIVES. WE CAN'T COMPLEMENT SOMEONE BY STARTING OUT WITH A NEGATIVE. IN THE SAME WAY, WE CAN'T TRULY PRAISE GOD AFTER WE FIRST COMPLAIN ABOUT OUR TROUBLES. GOD IS WORTHY OF OUR WORSHIP REGARDLESS OF OUR CIRCUMSTANCES. LET GOD CONTINUE TO WORK IN YOU TO PRODUCE A BEAUTIFUL MASTERPIECE. HE'S NOT FINISHED WITH US YET.

LIFE IS VERY GOOD!

"And he said: 'Naked I came from my mother's womb, And naked shall I return there. The LORD gave, and the LORD has taken away; Blessed be the name of the LORD' "(Job 1:21). Job knew more than anyone, what it was like to lose everything. He definitely had something to complain about. He lost his livestock, his cattle, his servants and his children all in one day. There was nothing Job did and there was nothing he could do about it. But the amazing thing was this: Job didn't complain. Instead, he gave God praise. Though he had all reason to "curse God and die" (Job 2:9), he had more reasons to praise the Lord. He felt he needed to accept the adversity, as well as the blessings. Job knew there had to be a greater purpose in what God was doing in his life.

Like Job, you may have much to complain about, but in reality there is something more happening than the trial going on in your life. Though you feel you have all rights and reasons to complain, what will that achieve? Will it make you feel better? Probably not. Will it bring your circumstances to an end? Complaining may actually make it feel as if it's taking longer. Complaining may cause you to lose hope. You cannot allow your troubles to get the best of you, because in the end, God can turn it around and do something wonderful in your life. The children of Israel complained time and time again about their situation and quickly forgot about all the wonders God had performed in their lives. Because of their complaining and stubbornness, a 3 day journey took 40 years, when all God wanted to do was take them into the Promised Land.

In John 5, there was a man who day after day laid at the pool of Bethesda. Jesus found out that he had been sick for 38 years, so he posed the man a question in verse 6: "Do you want to be made well?" Instead of answering the question, the man gave an excuse; in reality, he gave a complaint. "The sick man answered Him, 'Sir, I have no man to put me into the pool when the water is stirred up; but while I am coming, another steps down before me'" (John 5:7). The man's complaint was: I need help and no one is willing to help me. But on that day, Jesus was willing. Jesus wanted to do something in this man's life even though all he was concerned about was people's lack of assistance. When your complaint is greater than your praise, you will stay in the same condition season after season. There are many things you can be upset about, but there are many more things to be thankful for. Jesus, in His infinite compassion, saw past the man's excuses and healed him. You may not know why things happen the way they do, but know that God has a purpose in everything. Regardless of what is going on, lift up a thankful praise to the Lord. Complaining will only keep you stuck, but praise will break you through. Let God continue to do His work in your life.

The Lord says…

I cause the rain to fall on the just and the unjust in the same manner. I am no respecter of persons because I love all My children. Don't feel as if I'm mad at you because of your trials. I don't cause the trials, but sometimes I may allow them to cause your life to grow and flourish in the midst of it. Hardships can make you stronger, as long as you take My hand and let Me help you through it. Worship in every situation you encounter and don't let your complaint overtake your thinking. I have a purpose for your life; you are My masterpiece.

If you believe it, say oh yeah!

How long, O Lord? Will You forget me forever? How long will You hide Your face from me? How long shall I take counsel in my soul,

Having sorrow in my heart daily? How long will my enemy be exalted over me?

But I have trusted in Your mercy; My heart shall rejoice in Your salvation. I will sing to the Lord, Because He has dealt bountifully with me.

(Psalm 13:1-2, 5-6)

DAY 17
DON'T GET MAD, PRAISE!

When you feel overwhelmed by a situation, don't sit & do nothing. Let a praise & shout overwhelm your circumstance. Sometimes the best thing to do is laugh at what you can't control, remembering, He is always in control.

Life is very good!

There are times when you can feel like a deer in the headlights. You encounter a circumstance and it affects you to the point where you don't know what to do. You're frozen and the car is coming straight at you. What do you do? Do you stand there, allowing the circumstance to run over you? Or do you get up and out of the way?

There were 4 men in 2 Kings 7 who were in this type of situation. First of all, they were lepers so they had been exiled from the city because of their infirmity. Second, there was a famine in the entire region. Last, their country was at war with the Syrians. These 4 leprous men had nothing; they had no food, no money, and no home. In verse 3, they asked themselves, "Why are we sitting here until we die?" It was time for them to make a decision. They knew there was no food in the city, so going there would mean death, and staying where they were would also mean death. So they decided to do something different. "Now therefore, come, let us surrender to the army of the Syrians. If they keep us alive, we shall live; and if they kill us, we shall only die" (2 Kings 7:4). The odds were stacked against them. Yet instead of feeling helpless, they stood up and took control. They did SOMETHING instead of doing NOTHING. And God worked on their behalf. When these lepers arrived at the Syrian camp, no one was there. The Syrians had heard the sound of an army coming, of chariots and horses, and they fled. God took control of the situation and blessed the 4 lepers for taking a risk. Now they had "a day of good news" (verse 9) to share with everyone.

Your day might not start off in the best way. But as long as you don't do anything about it, it will stay that way. Instead, praise the Lord for the fact that you woke up. Praise Him for the job that you have. Thank Him for the raise you're praying for. Worship the Lord because your family has a place to live and food to eat. Do something different today. Don't get weary; sing a song. Don't get upset; put a smile on your face, even if you don't feel like it. There are so many things that are out of your control and that's ok. It's not out of God's control. So leave it in His hands and let Him take care of it. He will see you through.

The Lord says…

Don't feel burdened by your circumstances. I am the help you need. When things spin like a whirlwind around you, look up into the eye of the storm and you will see Me there. I see you. I know when you are hurting, when you are in pain, when you are overjoyed and when you are confused. I am the refuge to where you can run. Don't allow the cares of this world stop you from moving forward. I have your life in My hands and I will take care of you.

If you believe it, say oh yeah!

Hear my cry, O God; Attend to my prayer. From the end of the earth I will cry to You, When my heart is overwhelmed;

Lead me to the rock that is higher than I. For You have been a shelter for me, A strong tower from the enemy. I will abide in Your tabernacle forever; I will trust in the shelter of Your wings.

(Psalm 61:1-4)

DAY 18
WORSHIP THAT BREAKS THROUGH

In life, when we deal with issues, we are always searching for a way to break through to God to have Him help us overcome. The truth is, our worship causes God to break through to us. He is the Lord of the breakthrough. Let every day be a celebration of His victory in our lives.

Life is very good!

I think there are times we tend to overdo it when it comes to believing for a miracle. We look at verses like James 2:20 that says, "Faith without works is dead," and I believe that. I believe we need to have faith and 'work' for our breakthrough, whether it be by sowing a seed for your financial miracle or writing out a prophetic word and declaring it to manifest for your family. Yet people can get too caught up in doing all the works that they forget the simple things. You can't buy God's favor because it is His gift to us out of love; it's unmerited. Sometimes it just takes standing and knowing that He is God (Psalm 46:10) over every area of your life. That's where worship comes in. When you worship, pure and simple, you are reverencing God for who He is and the position He has in your life. He is the King of Kings and the Lord of Lords. Your declaration of God's greatness keeps Him in that place of honor and it shows Him that you are open for God to move in your life. When trials and tribulations occur, let your faith arise and submit all your troubles into His hands. By surrendering in worship, God can break through in your life and show His power.

In Matthew 9, starting in verse 18, the bible says one of the rulers of the synagogue came to see Jesus and worshiped Him. His name was Jairus, and his daughter was dying (cross-reference Luke 8:41). Jairus was so desperate that "he fell down at Jesus' feet" (Luke 8:41). This action was one of submission, surrender and worship before the Lord. He didn't care about the multitudes that surrounded Jesus. He didn't even care if any synagogue leaders saw him. What Jairus needed was a healing breakthrough for his daughter and his actions showed it. Jesus followed Jairus to his home where it was told that she had just died. But because Jairus had worshiped the Lord and believed in His power, the opportunity was there for a miracle. Jesus "took her by the hand and called, saying, 'Little girl, arise.' Then her spirit returned, and she arose immediately" (Luke 8:54-55). Breakthrough.

Matthew 8:2 shows a similar story of a leper who came and worshiped Jesus first before ever asking for healing. Jesus was willing and healed the man. Later in chapter 15, a Gentile woman cried out to Jesus for healing on behalf of her daughter. Even when she was insulted by Jesus, the woman still worshiped Him. Jesus saw her great faith and the desire of her heart within her worship, and healed her daughter. Breakthrough.

Take a lesson from these stories. It doesn't take a lot to grab the Lord's attention. All it takes is for you to surrender with your heart of worship. When you break through in worship, He'll break through to you and show you the victory in His Name.

The Lord says…

My desire is to be your provider, your help, your love, your all in all. When you call My Name, I hear you and will answer your cry. When you surrender, I know that your hope and trust is in Me, and I will be there in your time of need. I will break through on your behalf and show you My mercy, love and grace. I am your faithful God, the One who loves you.

If you believe it, say oh yeah!

Now when Daniel knew that the writing was signed, he went home. And in his upper room, with his windows open toward Jerusalem, he knelt down on his knees three times that day, and prayed and gave thanks before his God, as was his custom since early days…

Then Daniel said to the king, "O king, live forever! My God sent His angel and shut the lions' mouths, so that they have not hurt me, because I was found innocent before Him; and also, O king, I have done no wrong before you."

Now the king was exceedingly glad for him, and commanded that they should take Daniel up out of the den. So Daniel was taken up out of the den, and no injury whatever was found on him, because he believed in his God.

(Daniel 6:10, 21-23)

DAY 19
NO MORE LOOKING BACK

THE WAY TO MOVE FORWARD IS TO STOP LOOKING BACK. THE WAY TO RISE OVER A BAD SITUATION IS TO LET YOUR PRAISE BE GREATER THAN YOUR COMPLAINT. THE WAY TO OVERCOME ADVERSITY IS TO TRUST IN THE BLOOD OF THE LAMB & DECLARE THE WORD OF YOUR TESTIMONY. LET YOUR MOUTH BE FILLED WITH PRAISE AND LET YOUR WORDS BUILD UP THOSE AROUND YOU.

LIFE IS VERY GOOD!

You have probably read the story of Lot's wife in Genesis 19. As Lot, his wife and their daughters were fleeing Sodom and Gomorrah, Lot's wife decided to look back upon the city which was being destroyed and was turned into a pillar of salt. Even though she knew they had to escape the city, she still longed for that life. She couldn't move forward because her vision was on what was behind her, and it caused her to remain stuck in that place forever. Don't be like Lot's wife!

The past is gone and no matter what you do, it's not possible to reincarnate it today. You can't bring back the "glory days" of your youth, or even bring back a lost loved one. The only thing you can do is live in this moment, live in this day that God has granted you. Psalm 118:24 says, "This is the day the Lord has made; We will rejoice and be glad in it." The way you react to your life's circumstances today will have an effect on your tomorrow, so don't lift up a voice of complaint. Praise your way through your circumstances. When you rejoice and become glad for what the Lord has given you today, your outlook for tomorrow will be different. You won't look forward with dread or fear; you'll have hope that God has everything under control. You don't have to be afraid of your future. Let your words proclaim your trust in Him and what He holds for you. He isn't finished writing the book of your life.

Knowing that life wasn't over was especially important to Cory Hahn. On February 20, 2011, while playing only his 3rd college baseball game at Arizona State University, Hahn suffered a spinal cord injury while sliding head-first into second base. "I still think about it daily…because there's so many reminders… But I try not to dwell on it too much, because I realize it distracts me from what's really happening in life. You just lose focus." Hahn became a quadriplegic, paralyzed from his mid-chest to his toes yet he didn't allow his circumstance to deter his goals. After missing a year of school, he returned to ASU. Some semesters, he took more than 20 hours of classes in order to graduate with his class at Arizona State, which he eventually did. "Look, we all are going to deal with adversity, whether big or small, but it's not the adversity that defines who you are. It's how you handle it… And one day, one day, I want to stand up again, get out of that chair and walk."[5] Cory Hahn knew that complaining about what happened wasn't going to change it. The words he declares now encourages other people that face similar circumstances and is what helps propel Hahn forward to fulfill his dreams.

When you continually look behind you, you aren't able to focus on today. Things may have been difficult in the past, but that shouldn't hold you back from achieving your victory and grabbing hold of the blessings of God. Today is a new day for you. Praise God in the midst of all that is going on because His blood forgave and eradicated your past; it doesn't exist anymore! Let your testimony give glory to God and allow Him to advance you into greater things.

The Lord says...

I have you in My hands and Your future is in Me. Don't worry about what has happened to you or what you have done in the past. When you asked Me for forgiveness, I forgave you and placed your sin into the sea of forgetfulness and there it was erased. It is no more. My grace is enough for you. Take hold of today and do what I have called you to do, because your future is bright. Continue to praise Me in the midst of your circumstances and I will see you through. My Word will not return to Me void and I have already declared you to be victorious. Believe it and walk in it.

If you believe it, say oh yeah!

Not that I have already attained, or am already perfected; but I press on, that I may lay hold of that for which Christ Jesus has also laid hold of me. Brethren, I do not count myself to have apprehended; but one thing I do, forgetting those things which are behind and reaching forward to those things which are ahead, I press toward the goal for the prize of the upward call of God in Christ Jesus.

(Philippians 3:12-14)

5 Nightengale, Bob. "Even after Paralysis, Cory Hahn Finds Purpose in Baseball." *USA Today* (2015): 29 Mar. 2015. Web.

DAY 20
ATTITUDE ADJUSTMENT

A PERSON'S ATTITUDE TOWARDS A THING SHOULDN'T BE CHANGED BECAUSE OF WHAT ONE *HAS* TO DO, VERSES WHAT ONE *WANTS* TO DO. THE THINGS YOU DESIRE TO DO COME EASIER THAN THE THINGS THAT ARE NECESSARY TO DO. THE WORD PROCLAIMS, THE SPIRIT IS WILLING BUT THE FLESH IS WEAK. YOUR FLESH WILL ALWAYS CHOOSE THE EASIER. SO LET WORSHIP IGNITE YOUR SPIRIT TO ACCOMPLISH THE THINGS YOU DON'T FEEL LIKE DOING. SET YOUR PRIORITIES & MAKE THE DIFFICULT THINGS EASY.

LIFE IS VERY GOOD!

I have never been a morning person; I think it goes back to my time in college. Throughout the day, I had classes, lab and my job. So I got my homework done after all that was done, at night. When I had projects or reports to do, I would stay up late. When I had tests to study for, I would sometimes pull all-nighters. This 'schedule' then transitioned into my married life as we began ministering. Church services were normally in the evening, then we were usually taken out to eat. At first, I didn't have a job to go to during the week so it was easy to sleep in until 10 or 11am (Yes, I would sleep in that late). Then as the years passed and life changed, so my desire to sleep in had to also change.

Today I have 3 girls, who are always busy with something. After school, if it isn't dance class, it's voice class. If it isn't voice class, it's cheer practice. Along with that, I am the worship leader at the church we attend so not only am I early to church but I also have worship practice during the week. Plus we still have the traveling ministry. Needless to say, sleeping in is not a luxury I indulge in as often anymore (But thankfully, Rob does periodically take the girls to school so I can sleep until about 8am or so before we head to the gym). If I want to get things done, whether it be errands or housework or writing, I need to do get an early start.

Getting up early goes against what my physical body wants to do, but I have to push through if I intend to put my day to good use. What I want to do is always in conflict with what I need to do, and I cannot allow it to affect my attitude. Spiritually, it works the same way. Your spirit wants to be in communion with the Lord and sometimes in order to do that, you need to do things your flesh doesn't want to do. If you have children and your day is busy like mine, getting in your quiet time with God isn't easy. If I want to spend some quiet time with the Lord, I get up early and do my devotional time in the morning. It helps give me a wonderful perspective throughout my day. My body doesn't want to do it, but my spirit knows I need it. You may be one who does your devotional at lunch time. Your physical body wants to eat but your spiritual hunger is greater. So perhaps you take 15 minutes of your hour and spend it with God. He will honor your consistency and your commitment to Him.

Several times in the book of Psalms, King David had to exhort himself to praise the Lord (Psalm 25:1; 42:5, 11; 43:5, 103:2; 146:1). Even the one known as the "man after [God's] own heart" (1 Samuel 13:14), had to battle between his flesh and his spirit. David knew that what he needed to do outweighed what he wanted. He had the responsibility of the nation on his shoulders and it was more than he could handle on his own. He didn't complain when the Lord wanted to speak to him; David found it an honor that God chose him, a mere shepherd, to guide His people. He found it to be a necessity to worship the Lord, so his physical demands took a back seat.

Be sure to always make worship a priority in your life. Worshipers are the type of people God wants to work through because they have God's best interest at heart. Worshipers are the ones God uses to make a difference; He uses them to change the world! Are you that type of person? Are you a worshiper? If you have to wake up a little earlier, do it. If you have to stay up a little later, do it. Whatever sacrifice that needs to be made, God will honor it. He will make the difficult things easier, because nothing is as important as your lifestyle of worship to Him.

The Lord says…

I know some things are easier to do than others, but when you have My strength in you, all things are possible. Cry out to Me and I will be your help. Call out to Me and I will lift you up. I will make the tough things simpler, the impossible things possible, and the things you feel you cannot do, doable. I am on your side and will always be there for you. As long as you are willing to follow Me, I will be willing to guide you.

If you believe it, say oh yeah!

I cry out with my whole heart; Hear me, O Lord!
I will keep Your statutes. I cry out to You;
Save me, and I will keep Your testimonies.
I rise before the dawning of the morning,
And cry for help; I hope in Your word.

(Psalm 119:145-147)

DAY 21
PRAISE TO KEEP YOU GOING

THE STRUGGLE YOU FACE TODAY IS DEVELOPING THE STRENGTH YOU NEED FOR TOMORROW. LIFE MAY BE FILLED WITH PEAKS & VALLEYS BUT THEY DON'T DEFINE WHO YOU ARE. THEY JUST SAY WHERE YOU HAVE BEEN OR WHAT YOU HAVE LIVED THROUGH. YOUR LIFESTYLE & YOUR ATTITUDE TELLS ME WHO YOU ARE & WHERE YOU ARE GOING. KEEP YOUR SMILE & ALWAYS LIFT UP PRAISE. THEY WILL KEEP YOU STRONG.

LIFE IS VERY GOOD!

There is an illness that affects about 1-2% of the population called vitiligo. It is a disease that causes loss of skin color in blotches, most noticeable as patches of light colored skin all over the body. It is an interesting disease because there is no known cause nor a known cure. It isn't life threatening or contagious, and can happen to anyone. The reason I'm writing about this is because people who are affected by this disease tend to feel stressed, embarrassed or ashamed by how they look, even though they did nothing to bring on the disease. They may have a tendency to shy away from people for fear of being stared at. I saw a post on Instagram from someone who has vitiligo and she said, "There's no need to cry over the differences I have. All I know is I am never alone and God is my path. He shows me [the] way around the sadness; He helps me become stronger and fearless. I stand proud in my place, whether people like it or not. I may be different but that doesn't make me stop. People, like me, I know how you feel and I'm here to help you and show you God's will. God doesn't do things without a reason."

This young lady took authority over her illness and did not allow it to affect her. She did not let vitiligo define who she is today or who she will become tomorrow. The patches of skin color loss might have shown the scars of the illness, but her attitude showed the magnitude of her victory. The prophet Jeremiah wrote, "Heal me, O Lord, and I shall be healed; Save me, and I shall be saved, for you are my praise" (Jeremiah 17:14). Even Jeremiah suffered with circumstances that he couldn't take care of on his own. He prayed to God and continued to worship, knowing God was his salvation.

There may be an illness or situation you are dealing with, but you cannot allow it to take over your life. God created you for a reason and a purpose, though you may not see or understand what it is quite yet. You may have cancer but you are not a cancer patient. You may be battling depression but you are not a depressed person. You are who God declares you are: His child. Do not allow the trial to define you, let it be what drives you to gain victory. Let your praise declare what God is doing in your life. Though you may not feel victorious, the Victorious One lives in you. Others may see the scars you have on the outside, but that is only half the story. Let your lifestyle of worship declare where God has brought you from, but more importantly, where He is taking you.

The Lord says...

You have all you need to live an overcoming life. With Me living in you, there is nothing that can stop you from moving forward. Never allow the hardships of life to limit you or hold you down; your scars will become your battle wounds to push you to further victories. Remember, I also have scars. My hands and feet tell a story of unfailing love that will continue to speak until the end of time. I overcame death, hell and the grave to fill you with the strength to continue on this journey. Your circumstances don't define you; I have already declared who you are from the foundations of time. You are My child, in whom I am well pleased. Walk in that knowledge.

If you believe it, say oh yeah!

He sent His word and healed them, And delivered them from their destructions. Oh, that men would give thanks to the Lord for His goodness, And for His wonderful works to the children of men!

Let them sacrifice the sacrifices of thanksgiving,

And declare His works with rejoicing.

(Psalm 107:20-22)

DAY 22
CHANGE IT THROUGH WORSHIP

FRUSTRATED, TIRED AND DESIRE CHANGE? IF THIS IS YOU, YOU MUST BE AT YOUR WIT'S END. BREAKTHROUGH OFTEN HAPPENS WHEN YOU COME TO THE LAND OF "I DON'T CARE" OR "I QUIT". THIS BECOMES YOUR TIPPING POINT OF CHANGE WHERE YOUR POSTURE OF SURRENDERING BECOMES THE POINT OF TRANSFORMATION. INSTEAD OF THROWING UP YOUR HANDS IN DISGUST, LIFT THEM UP IN PRAISE & LET THIS BECOME A DEFINING MOMENT. YOUR SURRENDERING HAS TIPPED THE SCALES IN YOUR FAVOR, BELIEVE IT!

LIFE IS VERY GOOD!

It's easy to find yourself frustrated in the midst of trials and tribulations, but God doesn't want you stuck in that place. He knows you can rise above because of His strength in you. He's made you more than a conqueror because of His love for you (Romans 8:37). You need to allow His love to calm your heart, and allow His motivation to help push you forward. So many times because of dissatisfaction, you can find yourself so close to the edge of breakthrough but then stop short. You can't let that happen! Praise your way through!

There is always a defining moment in everyone's life; a point in time where you think, "Something has to change. I can't live this way. There has to be more." Jacob was at this point many times in his life. In Genesis 28, when Jacob had run away from Esau, God revealed Himself in a dream to reassure Jacob that He was with him. In Genesis 32, God revealed Himself in a more tangible manner by wrestling with Jacob throughout the night. Each time God spoke to Jacob, He reassured him of His promises and gave him a blessing. This was because Jacob had a lifestyle of worship and praised God no matter the circumstance surrounding him (Genesis 28:18-19; 32:30). He would constantly surrender his life unto the Lord and place it in God's hands, and at the end of every trial, Jacob would erect an altar unto the Lord or give an offering as a sign of thanksgiving. Jacob knew that on his own, he would fail, and he didn't want to remain stuck in that place of failure. God had too many promises for Jacob and his lineage, for him to give up.

Transformation will happen when you feel like you can't go on anymore. And it's at that point when God takes over. Your place of surrender becomes your place of change. Turn your situation around by praising your way through the trial. Your view on the circumstance will go from negative to positive because you will be seeing with His eyes and not your own. Your praise and worship will take you to a higher dimension if you allow it. That's because when you worship, you recognize and acknowledge God's worth in your life. You are exalting His character and your worship pays reverence unto the Lord. So in whatever frustrating situation you find yourself in, surrender, worship and praise God. Then He will transform your mind so you can experience your breakthrough.

The Lord says…

I know there will be times when you get frustrated. I know there will be times when you are sad. I know there will be times when you want to give up because the circumstances appear to be overwhelming. Just remember that during those times, I am with you. My promise is to never leave you nor forsake you. Lift up your voice of praise and see My hand move in your life and in your circumstance. Your transformation will happen when you fully surrender to Me and allow Me to work in your life. Don't worry My child; I have your life in My hands and I will never let you fall.

If you believe it, say oh yeah!

Then Jacob rose early in the morning, and took the stone that he had put at his head, set it up as a pillar, and poured oil on top of it. And he called the name of that place Bethel; but the name of that city had been Luz previously. Then Jacob made a vow, saying, "If God will be with me, and keep me in this way that I am going, and give me bread to eat and clothing to put on, so that I come back to my father's house in peace, then the Lord shall be my God. And this stone which I have set as a pillar shall be God's house, and of all that You give me I will surely give a tenth to You."

(Genesis 28:18-22)

DAY 23
DON'T REPEAT THE PAST

Do life's challenges have you on the run? If so, remember this: Running to Him is greater than running away. Just like worship is more than singing a song to Him, it's about positioning your heart before His presence. Your attitude in life is changed in worship. Bow your heart & lift up your voice today.

Life is very good!

We've heard the old adage: if you don't study history, you will be doomed to repeat it. The same bears true when you don't face your problems. It doesn't cause the problem to go away. The problem will be there until it gets dealt with. You might be able to shove it under the carpet for a while, but eventually it will find its way out again, and the next time around, it might be worse. So it's better to deal with it when it appears, and then move on.

When Jonah was told by the Lord to go to Nineveh, he chose not to. Instead, Jonah decided to board a boat in Joppa headed to Tarshish. Actually, Jonah fled from the presence of the Lord (Jonah 1:3). The word 'flee' in Hebrew means "to bolt, make haste, run away" (Strongs H1272). Jonah had some definite issues regarding going to Nineveh and he ran away like an olympic sprinter or a bat out of… well, you get the idea. God had a plan for the people of Nineveh but He wanted to give them a chance to repent. Jonah didn't think they deserved that chance (Jonah 4:1-2)

But running away from the Lord's command didn't cause the Lord to change it; it only made the situation worse for Jonah. While on the ship, the Lord sent a storm strong enough to tear the ship apart. The men tried to row to shore but the waves were too strong, so Jonah told them to throw him overboard. Immediately, "the sea ceased from its raging" (Jonah 1:15). Then Jonah got swallowed by a great fish, where he stayed for three days and nights. Finally, Jonah decided to pray, worship the Lord and follow His voice. "So the Lord spoke to the fish, and it vomited Jonah onto dry land" (Jonah 2:10).

How many times have you been like Jonah, running away from simple things that confront you? God wants you to turn to Him and not run away when times get tough. He's a merciful God and has a plan for your life. His heart is for His children. Position your heart toward Him and not on the problem because God has everything under control. Viewing it with your eyes will cause the situations to be magnified. Just do what Jonah did in verse 9 of chapter 2, "But I will sacrifice to You with the voice of thanksgiving." Give thanks to the Lord because He is good.

The Lord says…

I never want for you to run away from Me but to run to Me whenever life gets too overwhelming. Many times in My Word I say, “Come to Me, cry out to Me, pray to Me.” You are never alone whether in good times or in tough ones. I celebrate with you, I mourn with you, I am quiet with you. Know I am always here whenever you need Me. Run to Me.

If you believe it, say oh yeah!

Let my cry come before You, O Lord; Give me understanding according to Your word. Let my supplication come before You; Deliver me according to Your word. My lips shall utter praise, For You teach me Your statutes. My tongue shall speak of Your word, For all Your commandments are righteousness. Let Your hand become my help, For I have chosen Your precepts. I long for Your salvation, O Lord, And Your law is my delight. Let my soul live, and it shall praise You; And let Your judgments help me. I have gone astray like a lost sheep; Seek Your servant, For I do not forget Your commandments.

(Psalms 119:169-176)

DAY 24
POSITION YOUR HEART IN WORSHIP

WORSHIP IS MORE THAN LIFTING UP YOUR HANDS OR SINGING A SONG; IT'S ABOUT THE ATTITUDE OR POSITIONING OF YOUR HEART. IT'S TIME TO SURRENDER ALL TO HIM. TAKE UP MY YOKE FOR IT IS EASY & MY BURDEN, FOR IT IS LIGHT. IN THE ATMOSPHERE OF WORSHIP, EVERYTHING CHANGES.

LIFE IS VERY GOOD!

As a parent, I've seen my three daughters grow and mature into their own unique personality. Yet even as different as they are, they still have similarities. When something is difficult for the two older girls (a certain subject in school or a specific homework assignment), their attitude tends to get negative and often they'll say, "I don't like that class." We tell them to adjust their negative view of the class to a positive one and slowly things will begin to change.

We saw this exact thing happen with our oldest, Zoe. In 1st grade or so, she fell a bit behind in her reading levels and felt discouraged. She began to say she didn't like reading because it was too hard. We began to pray with her every morning before school and declared God's favor over her reading. We all worshiped and thanked Him for improved reading levels and comprehension. We helped her view the situation differently. We also taught her that she could worship and praise through any problem she went through. Soon after, Zoe found a book that caught her attention: Little House on the Prairie. She finished that book and checked out another in the series, and another, and another. Soon, her reading grades started improving to the point where her teacher asked us what we were doing differently. She asked if we got Zoe into tutoring or a specific reading program. We smiled and said, "We started praying every morning and thanking God for improved reading and comprehension." Her teacher, who was not a believer, replied with a smile, "Well, keep going because it's working."

The way you position your heart can change any situation you're in. Worship is the same. Anybody can sing a song or clap their hands, but it's the attitude of your worship that will change the atmosphere. John 4:23 says the "true worshipers will worship the Father in spirit and truth; for the Father is seeking such to worship Him." In spirit (not in the flesh or with your mind) and truth (honestly and not in ignorance). It shouldn't be a burden to worship God; it should be considered a privilege. Change your mindset and everything else will follow.

The Lord says…

I desire My people to worship without hesitation and without hindrance, for them to worship freely in spirit and in truth. But if your heart isn't positioned to worship, you will be distracted and allow other things to take your time. Spending time with you is important to Me, and I hope it's just as important to you. Don't burden yourself with meaningless things for I have destined you to live a blessed life.

If you believe it, say oh yeah!

Let the words of my mouth and the meditation of my heart
Be acceptable in Your sight, O Lord, my strength and my Redeemer.

(Psalm 19:14)

DAY 25
OBEDIENCE AS A FORM OF WORSHIP

In life, there are things God may ask of us that seem to be impossible. In these difficult times, walk in obedience. Abraham proclaimed, "The lad & I will come back to you," though Isaac was going to be sacrificed. Remember, there is no death in worship; it's a lifestyle that leads to His provision. Worship releases the power to overcome.

Life is very good!

As a parent of 3 beautiful girls, I always wonder if I would have been able to do the same thing Abraham was asked to do. It would be a difficult thing. God asked for a sacrifice from Abraham, but the offering required was not a lamb or dove; it was Isaac, Abraham's own son. Talk about a sacrifice of praise! Yet from the beginning, Abraham never questioned God's intention or complained. He always believed and obeyed. When God told him to leave his father's house, Abraham believed, obeyed and left (Genesis 12:1-4). When God told him to walk through the land He was giving him, Abraham believed, obeyed and moved his tent (Genesis 13:17-18), and because of his lifestyle of obedience, Abraham was accounted for as a righteous man (Genesis 15:6). Abraham's obedience was his form of worship. God saw that as a great thing, so in the end, Abraham didn't lose his son, he gained the provision and the full promise of God. When you give your best to God out of obedience to what He's asked, God will provide the exact thing you need. Abraham needed to show God that the promise he was given wasn't greater than the Giver of the promise.

God has given you all He has; all spiritual blessings have been made available to you because you are the seed of Abraham (Ephesians 1:3; Galatians 3:14,16). Therefore if God asked you for something, obedience to Him should be an easy thing because all you have belongs to God already. He freely gave to you as an example, that you may freely give back to Him. Obedience to God's Word should always be a part of your worship; it's what God asks of you and it's important to Him. And when you obey, it gives more rewards than you can possibly imagine. Don't think of a worship lifestyle as only singing and lifting up of your hands. Worship encompasses everything you do. When you listen to God's voice and follow His decrees, it's like a sweet aroma that rises up to His throne room. No matter how difficult life may get, continue to worship the Lord with your obedience. It will cause provision in your life that you didn't think was attainable, but yet everything you need.

The Lord says...

I have created you to worship. I have also created you with self-will. You are able to make your own decisions about who you will worship, about what you follow, about what you will obey. When you worship Me in spirit and in truth, I will bless you with everything I am and everything I have. I will pour My provision and grace over you to help you through the troublesome times in your life. In your worship, the only thing that dies is your flesh. Your spirit will rise to a new level in My Spirit and I will cause you to soar. Obedience will cause doors to open, for obedience is better than any sacrifice.

If you believe it, say oh yeah!

Therefore I urge you to reaffirm your love to him. For to this end I also wrote, that I might put you to the test, whether you are obedient in all things. Now whom you forgive anything, I also forgive. For if indeed I have forgiven anything, I have forgiven that one for your sakes in the presence of Christ.

(2 Corinthians 2:8-10)

DAY 26
WHY SO DOWNCAST OH MY SOUL?

THE WAY TO OVERCOME YOUR FRUSTRATION IN THE MIDST OF TROUBLE IS BY TAKING AUTHORITY OVER YOUR SOUL. COMMAND YOUR SOUL TO PRAY & SING, SO YOUR SPIRIT CAN AWAKEN. AS YOU DO THIS, YOUR HEAVINESS WILL LIFT & HIS JOY WILL PICK YOU UP. LIFT UP YOUR VOICE & SING TO THE BEAUTIFUL ONE. YOUR PRAISE WILL CHANGE EVERYTHING.

LIFE IS VERY GOOD!

Do you talk to yourself? I have a tendency to talk to myself sometimes and it makes Rob laugh. I tell him it helps me sort out my ideas or what I have to do for that day. The way I look at it is, if it helps me figure things out or get things done, I'm going to talk away! When I'm making better eating choices and my body is craving a candy bar, I tell myself to eat a protein bar instead. When my mind is trying to bombard me with frustrating thoughts, I tell my mind to cast out those thoughts, and then I do 'thank therapy'. Instead of my mind dwelling on thoughts that would upset me, I thank God for all the blessings He's given me. It turns my perspective around. There are times when Rob talks to himself as well. When he would run on the treadmill and felt like he couldn't run that last mile, I would hear him tell himself that he could do it.

This is exactly what the writer of Psalms 42 was doing. He felt the trials of life pressing in on him and his soul became distressed. He questioned himself in verse 5. "Why are you cast down, O my soul? And why are you disquieted within me?" Instead of succumbing to the pressure, he changed his outlook by telling his soul what to do: "Hope in God, for I shall yet praise Him for the help of His countenance." The psalmist had the recipe for overcoming in the palm of his hand, or more realistically, in his mouth. He began to place his hope in God and praise Him. Begin to do 'thank therapy' and praise the Lord for all He has done in your life. God's blessings far outweigh the petty frustrations that come along and you will feel better knowing God has given you much more than you realize. Remember weeping (frustration, anger, sadness) may endure for a night (just a short amount of time), but once you tell your soul to praise God, joy (unspeakable and full of glory) comes in the morning (a new day) (Psalm 30:5).

The Lord says...

There will come times of distress and frustration but those are but for a moment. My love, joy and peace are for a lifetime. Don't allow the stresses of life to weigh you down. I want to bless you because I love you and you are My child. Every time you speak to your soul to praise, it's really My voice rising up within you, giving you strength to overcome whatever you are struggling with. Put your hope, trust and faith in Me and I will see you through. I will carry your burden and walk with you to the end.

If you believe it, say oh yeah!

Praise the LORD! Praise the LORD, O my soul! While I live I will praise the LORD; I will sing praises to my God while I have my being.

(Psalms 146:1-2)

DAY 27
DON'T REMIND ME

When the adversary tries to shame you of your past, shame that lying devil back by lifting your hand, praising God and glorifying Him through worship. God is greater than the lie you have been told, & He is able to deliver you out of your situation. Victory is discovered in your praise! Rise up with your shout.

Life is very good!

There is a simplicity in worship. It's all about taking your eyes off yourself and your circumstance and focusing on the Lord and who He is. When you can do that, all else fades into the background: your problems, your trials, your sickness, your past, everything. It doesn't mean that all those things will go away; it just means they aren't in the forefront of your thinking. The Lord has become the priority. When you can focus on the Lord in worship, it will change your mindset and you will see your life in a different manner. The way you approach circumstances will change because you're relying on God instead of what you used to do: rely on yourself.

Zacchaeus was a man who tended to rely on himself. He had to; he was a tax collector during Jesus' time. He was hated by the people and viewed as a sinner by the religious sector. But there was something within Zacchaeus that wanted more out of life and when he heard Jesus was passing through his town, he wasn't going to allow the opportunity to pass him by. Zacchaeus knew where Jesus was going to pass so he climbed a tree and waited. Luke 19:5 says, "And when Jesus came to the place, He looked up and saw him, and said to him, 'Zacchaeus, make haste and come down, for today I must stay at your house.'" The following verse says that Zacchaeus received Jesus joyfully. Not only did he receive Him as a guest in his physical home, Zacchaeus received Jesus spiritually into his heart. His past was washed away. But immediately everyone complained and gossiped about Zacchaeus being a sinner. They probably said many more things along with that in order to shame and embarrass him, yet Zacchaeus was not deterred. He relied on his new-found relationship with Jesus and stood on that. Jesus coming into his life was so powerful and profound that he turned and told Jesus he would give half of what he had to the poor and would restore 4-fold to those he took from by false accusation (Luke 19:6-8). Jesus knew this was a true act of worship. Salvation had come to Zacchaeus and nothing anyone said could change that. Zacchaeus knew he had a past, but now he had a new future and wouldn't allow anyone to steal his worship. Victory was his! Stand on the foundation of your relationship with Christ, and when others (or the adversary) try to remind you of who you used to be, just let them know who you are now: a child of the Most High God; saved, forgiven and redeemed.

The Lord says…

You are My child and I love you with more love than you realize. I gave My life to save you from an eternity of hell. Because you have received Me into your life, your heart was transformed and your life took on a whole new meaning. Don't worry about what others will say; their words don't matter. The only thing that truly matters is My Word and what that Word speaks about you. I gave you life. I gave you healing. I gave you hope. I gave you truth. On those things, and much more, you can rely. Continue to worship because it will give you victory for each day and strength to stand against any accusations.

If you believe it, say oh yeah!

Bless the LORD, O my soul; And all that is within me, bless His holy name! Bless the LORD, O my soul, And forget not all His benefits: Who forgives all your iniquities, Who heals all your diseases, Who redeems your life from destruction, Who crowns you with lovingkindness and tender mercies, Who satisfies your mouth with good things, So that your youth is renewed like the eagle's.

For as the heavens are high above the earth, So great is His mercy toward those who fear Him; As far as the east is from the west, So far has He removed our transgressions from us.

(Psalms 103:1-5, 11-12)

DAY 28
IN PRAISE, ANYTHING IS POSSIBLE

REMEMBER THIS: THE CHAINS THAT ONCE HELD YOU IN BONDAGE, ONCE YOU'VE BEEN SET FREE, BECOME AN INSTRUMENT FOR HIS PRAISE. GOD CAN USE ALL THINGS TO MAKE A SOUND OF WORSHIP. REJOICE IN HIS FREEDOM.

LIFE IS VERY GOOD!

I enjoy movies. Anyone who really knows me knows this to be true. A particular scene came to mind after I wrote this entry and I thought it fit perfectly, so I decided to add it in. It's toward the end of *Saving Mr. Banks* (2013, Disney) where Mrs. Travers is taken to the airport by her driver, Ralph. After she autographs his daughter Jane's copy of *Mary Poppins*, she hands him a slip of paper.

Mrs. Travers: Now take this.

Ralph: (He reads the paper.) Albert Einstein, Van Gogh, Roosevelt, Frida Kahlo… What is this?

Mrs. Travers: They all have difficulties. Jane can do anything that anyone else can do.

Do you understand?

Ralph: (He nods his head in acknowledgment as his eyes well with tears.)

Ralph had explained to Mrs. Travers earlier in the movie that Jane was in a wheelchair and couldn't do many of the things other children did. She let him know that it didn't matter the difficulty, there was nothing that kept all those famous people from following their dreams, and the same was true for his daughter. It is also true for you.

Take your disability and turn it into an ability. Take what was impossible and make it possible. These sayings are encouraging because they let you know that whatever was holding you back, you can still use it to bring out something positive. Many preachers use these sayings as well: "Turn your mess into your message" or "Turn your test into your testimony". They all carry the same theme: you can do anything you set your mind to, no matter what. Praise the Lord in all circumstances because He has set you free from the bondage of sin.

My nephew Ruben was the type of person that never took 'no' for an answer. When he had a goal in his heart, he made sure to carry it out. When he wanted to make changes to the sound room at the church, he made his plans known to his dad, the pastor. When he wanted to make the church flyers and website more eye-catching, he took computer classes at the local college. When a guest minister came to the church and he wanted to be ministered to, Ruben made sure he was at the altar. It didn't matter that he was born with spina bifida and in a wheelchair because he was paralyzed from the waist down. It didn't matter that the doctors said he would never walk. He wouldn't allow a sickness that physically hindered his body to spiritually hinder him. He would praise and worship with the rest of us. He would wheel around everywhere we went and would not be left behind. Even when he contracted an infection that slowly took away his strength, Ruben never stopped thanking the Lord. He knew his entire life was a miracle and he had a reason to worship. And on the day the Lord took him home on August 9, 2012, the physical chains that tried to hold him down were completely broken. His spiritual freedom manifested into a physical one and his spirit was united forever with his Heavenly Father.

Ruben's life holds an important lesson that everyone can learn and it's found in John 8:36, "Therefore if the Son makes you free, you shall be free indeed." Chains, which can be physical, spiritual, mental or emotional, can keep you from pursuing the greater call God has for your life. Once you start telling yourself, "I can't do that," the chains will get stronger and tighter. The Son of God gave His life so you can live in His freedom. There is nothing holding you back anymore! What greater message is there? Worship the Lord and thank Him for what He's done for you. Ruben couldn't use his legs to dance, so he used his arms to clap and his voice to sing. God can use anything to become an instrument for His glory. Rejoice in what He's given you and know you have been made free.

The Lord says...

Don't ever see your shortcomings as limitations because I see them differently. You have been created in My image and My likeness. You look like your Father. Take the gifts and talents I have placed in your life and use them as a tool to bring others into the Kingdom. What others see as limitations, use them as an advantage. You have been set apart to do something great. Believe it and receive it this day.

If you believe it, say oh yeah!

Then Moses said to the Lord, "O my Lord, I am not eloquent, neither before nor since You have spoken to Your servant; but I am slow of speech and slow of tongue."

So the Lord said to him, "Who has made man's mouth? Or who makes the mute, the deaf, the seeing, or the blind? Have not I, the Lord? Now therefore, go, and I will be with your mouth and teach you what you shall say."

So the people believed; and when they heard that the Lord had visited the children of Israel and that He had looked on their affliction, then they bowed their heads and worshiped.

(Exodus 4:10-12, 31)

DAY 29
JESUS WAS A LIFESTYLE OF WORSHIP

JESUS WAS A SACRIFICIAL LAMB THAT ALLOWED HIS LIFE TO BE PLAYED AS AN INSTRUMENT OF WORSHIP TO BRING GLORY TO HIS FATHER AND REDEMPTION TO MANKIND. THE SOUND OF HIS SUFFERING WAS A BEAUTIFUL SONG TO THE HEAVENS THAT FREED US ALL. LIVE IN HIS FREEDOM TODAY.

LIFE IS VERY GOOD!

When you worship someone or something, you give all of yourself in reverence and honor to that object. You respect what you worship because it holds importance in your life. So, in looking at it from that aspect, the ultimate example of true worship was Jesus Christ Himself. Jesus held His relationship with His Father in such high regard that He obeyed the Father's instruction to go to the cross. He could have chosen differently but Jesus followed the path set before Him. His obedience was His worship. It was more than singing, it was more than lifting His hands, it was more than giving an offering; Jesus allowed His lifestyle of obedience to the Father to be the worship that sprung from His Spirit. Along with that, Christ loved us so much so that He gave Himself as a sacrifice in our place. For true redemption to take place, it was going to take a perfect offering. Humans aren't perfect, and we will never be. Only Jesus as the Lamb of God was able to make the redemption of our sins a reality.

Ephesians 5:2 says, "And walk in love, as Christ also has loved us and given Himself for us, an offering and a sacrifice to God for a sweet-smelling aroma." An offering is something that is freely given out of the love in your heart. Jesus gave Himself as an offering because He loved His Father and us, but He was also a sacrifice, which means it wasn't easy for Him to do. True worship is an offering and a sacrifice; it's when you are willing to give yourself completely to your Heavenly Father, even when times are difficult or when it's not convenient. It is in those times when worship is the most special to the heart of God. Hannah cried out to God wanting a child in 1 Samuel 1:10-11. She lifted up a prayer that came directly from the depths of her heart. God received her worship and gave her a son, Samuel (1 Samuel 1:20). In Luke 7:37-38, there was a woman who broke open her alabaster flask of oil and anointed the feet of Jesus as an act of worship. Not only was that a sacrifice for her (the oil was worth a year's wages), but the act itself was not done at a convenient time. There were many at the house where Jesus was, and they all knew she was a 'sinner'. Despite their disdain and condemnation, this woman not only poured out of her livelihood, but she poured out of herself. Both these women did what Jesus did: gave an offering and sacrifice of worship to the Lord because they loved. It was a sweet song that was played in the throne room of heaven. These acts of true worship brought freedom to these women's lives just as what Jesus did opened the door for you to be able to walk in that same freedom.

You don't have to live in worry or fear the future. You don't have to live in condemnation because of how you lived your life in the past. The past is gone and you are free in Him today. Jesus' worship made that possible. Your worship should be the same. When you truly worship the Lord, it should open doors for others to worship with you. It should help people feel the same type of freedom. Let your life be a beautiful song unto the King and every day, remember to live the way you worship, in freedom.

The Lord says…

To Me, worship is more than a song; it's complete surrender in My presence, and that's what I love to see. I love when you cry out to Me. I love to hear your voice. I love to see your tears. I know when you kneel at My altar and lay your life down at My feet, it's coming directly from your heart. I receive that worship because I know it comes as a sacrifice. Life isn't easy but you continue to worship knowing I am with you. The winds will blow but I am the shelter covering you. I gave My life to set you free and it pleases Me to see you walking in My joy. Let every day be a new experience in My presence, for I am like the sun that shines upon you during the day and the moon that stands with you even in the dark times. Always let your life be a life of worship that honors Me and brings others into a realm of freedom they've never experienced before.

If you believe it, say oh yeah!

Now Araunah said to David, "Let my lord the king take and offer up whatever seems good to him. Look, here are oxen for burnt sacrifice, and threshing implements and the yokes of the oxen for wood. All these, O king, Araunah has given to the king."

And Araunah said to the king, "May the Lord your God accept you."

Then the king said to Araunah, "No, but I will surely buy it from you for a price; nor will I offer burnt offerings to the Lord my God with that which costs me nothing." So David bought the threshing floor and the oxen for fifty shekels of silver. And David built there an altar to the Lord, and offered burnt offerings and peace offerings. So the Lord heeded the prayers for the land, and the plague was withdrawn from Israel.

(2 Samuel 24:22-25)

DAY 30
LET YOUR WORSHIP GO ABOVE AND BEYOND

When you exalt the Lord, your praise opens the door to increase. Remember, whatever you celebrate becomes magnified in your life. Lift up a shout and allow God to provide what you need. He is El-Shaddai, the God of more than enough. Praise your way to provision today!

Life is very good!

When you take a stand for something, people notice. Just look at Shadrach, Meshach and Abed-Nego in Daniel 3. While everyone bowed down to the image of gold King Nebuchadnezzar had made, these three young men didn't. They took a stand for what they believed in and Who they believed in. To everyone, their stance was ridiculous. Going against the king's decree would mean death. In the eyes of Nebuchadnezzar, it was maddening. He couldn't believe they thought there was someone greater and more worthy of worshiping. But Shadrach, Meshach and Abed-Nego had seen enough miracles in their lives to know God would protect them from the fiery furnace. And even if He didn't, they wouldn't go against their convictions. They celebrated who God was in their lives and in doing this, God provided what they needed: protection. God shielded them from the flames and even went beyond that. When the furnace was heated "seven times more than it was usually heated" (Daniel 3:19), those who threw them into the furnace were killed but Shadrach, Meshach and Abed-Nego were untouched. "The fire had no power; the hair of their head was not singed nor were their garments affected, and the smell of fire was not on them" (verse 27). In the end, even King Nebuchadnezzar had to admit to the power of God that he himself saw. And Shadrach, Meshach and Abed-nego were "promoted…in the province of Babylon" (verse 30). When you praise the Lord, He will come through for you. You will see His hand move and provide what you need, going above and beyond.

Worship can do so much for you. It causes you to know God in a deeper way (Psalm 76:1). It causes bondages to break off your life and others (Acts 16:25-26). It makes you realize how much God thinks about you, how much He loves you and how He wants to bless you (Psalm 91:14-16). God is faithful to His Word, and when you praise and worship Him, it empowers His Word in a greater manner.

Abraham and Job were two men who knew God's faithfulness and saw it first-hand. Their lives were about completely trusting and having faith in God. They followed Him whole-heartedly and were blessed because of it. Abraham received promises time and time again from God regarding his legacy and how he would be the father of many nations (Genesis 12:2,7; 13:15; 15:3). Job, in the midst of all he went through, chose not to be angry with God about his circumstances, and in the end, received double of all that he previously had (Job 42:10). Abraham and Job had something in common: they had a lifestyle of worship. When God spoke, they listened and obeyed, even when it meant sacrificing what they loved the most (Genesis 22:2). And when God poured out, they were thankful and worshiped. Everywhere God led Abraham in his journey, he set up altars and praised the Lord. Job sacrificed on behalf of himself and his children. They both took a stand for righteousness and people took notice. Even the devil himself commented about how much protection Job had on his life (Job 1:9-10). When you proclaim how great God is in your life, He will show Himself great on your behalf. He wants to be your provision and meet all of your needs. All you need to do is have a lifestyle of worship and the rest will fall into place. Celebrate who He is and He will be more than enough for you.

The Lord says…

I am Jehovah Jireh, the Lord your provider. I am El-Shaddai, the God of more than enough. I am Jehovah Nissi, the God of victory. And because I abide in you, you are victorious as well. Your life can prosper and flourish because you believe in what I can do through you. I need you as My chosen vessel on this earth. When you praise Me, I will open doors for you that were closed before. When you worship Me, I can move the mountains that were standing as obstacles in your path. I am all that you need, now and forever.

If you believe it, say oh yeah!

Now to Him who is able to do exceedingly abundantly above all that we ask or think, according to the power that works in us, to Him be glory in the church by Christ Jesus to all generations, forever and ever. Amen.

(Ephesians 3:20-21)

REFERENCES

1. Munroe, Myles. Potential for Every Day. Shippensburg, PA: Destiny Image, 2008. Print.

2. Mayo Clinic Staff. “Stress Management.” Positive Thinking: Reduce Stress by Eliminating Negative Self-talk. Mayo Clinic, 4 March, 2014. Web.

3. “Dictionary.com - The World’s Favorite Online English Dictionary!” Dictionary.com. 2016. Web.

4. The Help. Dreamworks, 2011. Film.

5. Nightengale, Bob. “Even after Paralysis, Cory Hahn Finds Purpose in Baseball.” USA Today (2015): 29 Mar. 2015. Web.

To find more resources by Prophet Rob Sanchez Ministries
Visit: www.prophetrobsanchez.com

Get more of Prophets Rob's #LIVG quotes daily by following on
Facebook (facebook.com/ProphetRobSanchez)
& Twitter (@prophetrobpfi)

If you have a book and would like to publish
with Firstfruits Publishing, contact us at:
firstfruitspublishing@prophetrobsanchez.com